A Prayer Treasury

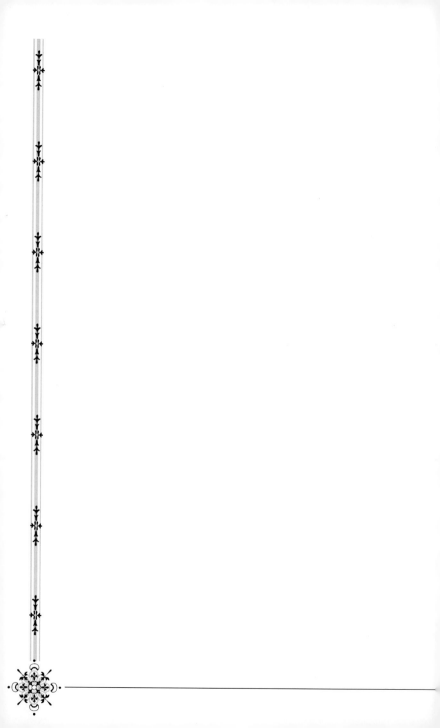

This edition copyright © 1998 Lion Publishing

Published by
Lion Publishing plc
Sandy Lane West, Oxford, England
www.lion-publishing.co.uk
ISBN 0 7459 3933 3
First edition 1998
10 9 8 7 6

A catalogue record for this book is available
from the British Library

Printed and bound in Singapore

A Prayer
Treasury

A LION BOOK

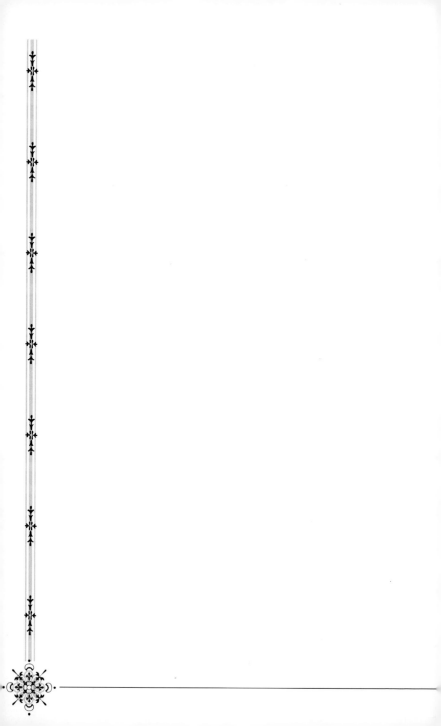

CONTENTS

PART ONE: CLASSIC PRAYERS

PART TWO: PRAYERS FOR EVERY OCCASION

INTRODUCTION

The practice of prayer is as old as humanity itself. To be alive and to have some sense of the presence of God, is to pray. Human beings have shared this experience throughout our recorded history and it is no surprise that a rich heritage of written prayers has come down to us.

This collection brings together some of the best known and loved of these prayers, from the ancient blessings of the Old Testament to Gerard Manley Hopkins' beautiful prayer poem, 'Pied Beauty'. To pray using these time-honoured words, is to join with those who have gone before us in approaching the same loving God with our own petitions and needs.

The second half of the collection provides prayers for every occasion. The first sections contain words with which to approach God, words of praise and of thanksgiving. These are followed by a wide variety of petitions and requests for ourselves and for our world. There are prayers for private use and for public occasions, for all the major seasonal celebrations and for those special family rites of passage that bring us all closer to God – from the joy and wonder at the arrival of a new baby to the need to find words at a bereavement.

Helping children to learn the art of prayer is important. A special section of best-loved children's prayers has been included, together with graces and blessings.

This treasury is designed to be a continuous source of strength and encouragement, joy and enrichment and to provide a link between the needs of our own day and the rich heritage of prayer.

PART ONE

CLASSIC PRAYERS

THE LORD'S PRAYER

*When Jesus' disciples asked him to teach them to pray,
his response was to give them a prayer as an example.
It has become known as the Lord's Prayer and is the
best known and most widely used Christian prayer in
the world. This is the traditional version from The Book
of Common Prayer.*

Our Father,
which art in heaven,
hallowed be thy name.
Thy kingdom come.
Thy will be done, in earth as it is in heaven.
Give us this day our daily bread.
And forgive us our trespasses,
as we forgive them that trespass against us.
And lead us not into temptation;
but deliver us from evil:
for thine is the kingdom,
the power, and the glory,
for ever and ever.

BASED ON THE BOOK OF MATTHEW, CHAPTER 6

This modern version is now accepted by a wide variety of Christian groups worldwide.

Our Father in heaven,
hallowed be your name,
your kingdom come,
your will be done on earth as in heaven.
Give us today our daily bread.
Forgive us our sins
as we forgive those who sin against us.
Save us from the time of trial
and deliver us from evil.
For the kingdom, the power and the glory are yours
now and for ever.

<small>Version from the English Language Liturgical Commission</small>

BEST-KNOWN PRAYERS

This section contains some of the best-known prayers, drawn from the Old Testament and 2,000 years of Christian history.

The shepherd psalm

The Lord is my shepherd;
I shall not want.
He maketh me to lie down in green pastures:
    he leadeth me beside the still waters.
He restoreth my soul:
    he leadeth me in the paths of righteousness
    for his name's sake.
Yea, though I walk through the valley of the
    shadow of death,
I will fear no evil:
    for thou art with me;
    thy rod and thy staff they comfort me.
Thou preparest a table before me
    in the presence of mine enemies:
    thou anointest my head with oil;
    my cup runneth over.
Surely goodness and mercy shall follow me
    all the days of my life:
    and I will dwell in the house of the Lord for ever.

FROM THE BOOK OF PSALMS, CHAPTER 23, ATTRIBUTED TO KING DAVID

A cry for help

As a deer longs for flowing streams,
so my soul longs for you, O God.
My soul thirsts for God, for the living God.
When shall I come and behold the face of God?
My tears have been my food day and night,
while people say to me continually,
'Where is your God?'

These things I remember,
as I pour out my soul:
how I went with the throng,
and led them in procession to the house of God,
with glad shouts and songs of thanksgiving,
a multitude keeping festival.

Why are you cast down, O my soul,
and why are you disquieted within me?
Hope in God; for I shall again praise him,
my help and my God.

FROM THE BOOK OF PSALMS, CHAPTER 42

Mary's song

*Sometimes called the Magnificat, after the first word
in the Latin translation, this is the song of Mary the
mother of Jesus upon visiting her cousin Elizabeth with
the news of her pregnancy.*

My soul magnifies you, my Lord,
    and my spirit rejoices in God my Saviour,
    for you have looked with favour
    on the lowliness of your servant.
You, the Mighty One, have done great things for me,
    and holy is your name.
Your mercy is for those who fear you
    from generation to generation.
You have scattered the proud in the thoughts
    of their hearts.
You have brought down the powerful from their thrones,
    and lifted up the lowly.
You have filled the hungry with good things,
    and sent the rich away empty.

BASED ON THE GOSPEL OF LUKE, CHAPTER 1

Evening prayer

Watch, dear Lord,
with those who wake,
or watch, or weep tonight,
and give your angels charge
over those who sleep.
Tend your sick ones, O Lord Christ,
rest your weary ones.
Bless your dying ones.
Soothe your suffering ones.
Pity your afflicted ones.
Shield your joyous ones.
And all for your love's sake.

St Augustine of Hippo, fifth century

Te Deum Laudamus

We praise thee, O God:

   we acknowledge thee to be the Lord.

All the earth doth worship thee, the Father everlasting.

To thee all angels cry aloud, the heavens,

   and all the powers therein.

To thee Cherubin, and Seraphin continually do cry,

Holy, Holy, Holy:

Lord God of Sabaoth;

Heaven and earth are full of the majesty of thy glory.

The glorious company of the apostles praise thee.

The goodly fellowship of the prophets praise thee.

The noble army of martyrs praise thee.

The holy Church throughout all the world doth

   acknowledge thee;

   the Father of an infinite majesty;

   thine honourable, true and only Son;

   also the Holy Ghost, the Comforter.

A FOURTH-CENTURY HYMN

St Patrick's Breastplate

Known as St Patrick's Breastplate, this ancient Irish hymn was translated in the nineteenth century by Mary Byrne and written in verse form by Eleanor Hull.

I bind unto myself today
the power of God to hold and lead,
his eye to watch, his might to stay,
his ear to hearken to my need.
The wisdom of my God to teach,
his hand to guide, his shield to ward;
the Word of God to give me speech,
his heavenly host to be my guard.

Christ be with me, Christ within me,
Christ behind me, Christ before me,
Christ beside me, Christ to win me,
Christ to comfort and restore me,
Christ beneath me, Christ above me,
Christ in quiet, Christ in danger,
Christ in hearts of all that love me,
Christ in mouth of friend and stranger.

ATTRIBUTED TO ST PATRICK

Eternal God

Eternal God,
the light of the minds that know you,
the life of the souls that love you,
the strength of the wills that serve you;
help us so to know you that we may truly love you,
so to love you that we may fully serve you,
whom to serve is perfect freedom.

POPE GELASIUS' PRAYER BOOK, SEVENTH OR EIGHTH CENTURY

Into your hands

Into your hands, O Lord and Father, we commend our souls and bodies, our parents and our homes, friends and servants, neighbours and kindred, our benefactors and departed brethren, all your people faithfully believing and all who need your pity and protection. Enlighten us with your holy grace and suffer us never more to be separated from you, one God in Trinity, God everlasting.

EDMUND OF ABINGDON, THIRTEENTH CENTURY

An instrument of your peace

Lord make me an instrument of your peace.
Where there is hatred, let me sow love;
where there is injury, pardon;
where there is discord, union;
where there is doubt, faith;
where there is despair, hope;
where there is darkness, light;
where there is sadness, joy.

O Divine Master, grant that I may not so much seek
to be consoled as to console;
to be understood as to understand;
to be loved, as to love;
for it is in giving that we receive,
it is in pardoning that we are pardoned,
and it is in dying that we are born to eternal life.

A PRAYER ATTRIBUTED TO ST FRANCIS OF ASSISI

Be thou my vision

Be thou my vision, O Lord of my heart,
be all else but naught to me, save that thou art;
be thou my best thought in the day and the night,
both waking and sleeping, thy presence my light.

Be thou my wisdom, be thou my true word;
be thou ever with me, and I with thee, Lord;
be thou my great Father, and I thy true son;
be thou in me dwelling, and I with thee one.

Be thou my breastplate, my sword for the fight;
be thou my whole armour, be thou my true might;
be thou my soul's shelter, be thou my strong tower,
O raise thou me heavenward, great Power of my power.

Riches I heed not, nor man's empty praise,
be thou mine inheritance now and always,
be thou and thou only the first in my heart;
O Sovereign of heaven, my treasure thou art.

High King of heaven, thou heaven's bright Sun,
O grant me its joys, after victory is won;
Great Heart of my own heart, whatever befall,
still be thou my vision, O Ruler of all.

ANCIENT IRISH HYMN

A *life to proclaim thee*

O gracious and holy Father,
give us wisdom to perceive thee,
intelligence to understand thee,
diligence to seek thee,
patience to wait for thee,
eyes to behold thee,
a heart to meditate upon thee,
and a life to proclaim thee;
through the power of the spirit
of Jesus Christ our Lord.

ATTRIBUTED TO ST BENEDICT OF NURSIA, SIXTH CENTURY

My *safety*

Alone with none but thee, my God,
I journey on my way.
What need I fear, when thou art near,
O King of night and day?
More safe am I within thy hand
than if a host did round me stand.

St Columba of Iona, sixth century

My *druid is Christ*

My Druid is Christ, the son of God,
Christ, Son of Mary, the Great Abbot,
The Father, the Son, and the Holy Ghost.

Attributed to St Columba of Iona, sixth century

Friend and brother

Thanks be to thee,
Lord Jesus Christ,
for all the benefits
which thou hast won for us,
for all the pains and insults
which thou hast borne for us.

O most merciful redeemer, friend and brother,
may we know thee more clearly,
love thee more dearly,
and follow thee more nearly,
day by day.

RICHARD OF CHICHESTER, THIRTEENTH CENTURY

To do God's will

Teach me to serve thee as thou deservest;
to give and not to count the cost,
to fight and not to heed the wounds,
to toil and not to seek for rest,
to labour and not to seek reward,
save that of knowing that I do thy will.

IGNATIUS OF LOYOLA, SIXTEENTH CENTURY

A prayer of surrender

Take, Lord, all my liberty,
my memory, my understanding,
and my whole will.
You have given me all that I have,
all that I am,
and I surrender all to your divine will,
that you dispose of me.
Give me only your love and your grace.
With this I am rich enough,
and I have no more to ask.

IGNATIUS OF LOYOLA, SIXTEENTH CENTURY

God be in my head

God be in my head
and in my understanding;
God be in my eyes
and in my looking;
God be in my mouth
and in my speaking;
God be in my heart
and in my thinking;
God be at my end
and at my departing.

BOOK OF HOURS, SIXTEENTH CENTURY

Collect for aid against all perils

Lighten our darkness, we beseech thee, O Lord; and by thy great mercy defend us from all perils and dangers of this night; for the love of thy only son, our Saviour, Jesus Christ.

FROM THE BOOK OF COMMON PRAYER

Collect for Ash Wednesday

Almighty and everlasting God, who hatest nothing that thou hast made, and dost forgive the sins of all them that are penitent; create and make in us new and contrite hearts, that we, worthily lamenting our sins, and acknowledging our wretchedness, may obtain of thee, the God of all mercy, perfect remission and forgiveness; through Jesus Christ our Lord.

FROM THE BOOK OF COMMON PRAYER

Christ's body

Christ has no body now on earth but yours;
yours are the only hands with which he can do his work,
yours are the only feet with which he can go about the world,
yours are the only eyes through which his compassion
can shine forth upon a troubled world.
Christ has no body now on earth but yours.

ST TERESA OF AVILA, SIXTEENTH CENTURY

Deliver us

From silly devotions
and from sour-faced saints,
good Lord, deliver us.

ST TERESA OF AVILA, SIXTEENTH CENTURY

Fear no more

Wilt thou forgive that sin where I begun,
which was my sin, though it were done before?
Wilt thou forgive that sin, through which I run,
and do run still: though still I do deplore?
When thou hast done, thou hast not done,
for I have more.

Wilt thou forgive that sin by which I have won
others to sin, and made my sin their door?
Wilt thou forgive that sin which I did shun
a year, or two; but wallowed in, a score?
When thou hast done, thou hast not done,
for I have more.

I have a sin of fear, that when I've spun
my last thread, I shall perish on the shore;
Swear by thyself that at my death thy Son
shall shine – as he shines now, and heretofore;
and, having done that, thou hast done,
I fear no more.

John Donne, seventeenth century

Contentment

He that is down needs fear no fall,
he that is low, no pride:
he that is humble ever shall,
have God to be his guide.

I am content with what I have,
little be it or much:
and, Lord, contentment still I crave,
because thou savest such.

JOHN BUNYAN, SEVENTEENTH CENTURY

Dappled things

Glory be to God for dappled things –
for skies of couple-colour as a brinded cow;
for rose-moles all in stipple upon trout that swim;
fresh-firecoal chestnut-falls; finches' wings;
landscape plotted and pierced-fold, fallow, and plough;
and all trades, their gear and tackle and trim.
All things counter, original, spare, strange;
whatever is fickle, freckled (who knows how?)
with swift, slow; sweet, sour; adazzle, dim;
he fathers-forth whose beauty is past change:
praise him.

GERARD MANLEY HOPKINS, NINETEENTH CENTURY

Acceptance and change

God, give us grace to accept with serenity
the things that cannot be changed,
courage to change the things that should be changed,
and the wisdom to distinguish the one from the other.

REINHOLD NIEBUHR, TWENTIETH CENTURY

The bundle of life

O God, you have bound us together in this bundle of life;
give us grace to understand how our lives depend on the
courage, the industry, the honesty and integrity of our fellow
men; that we may be mindful of their needs, grateful for their
faithfulness, and faithful in our responsibilities to them; through
Jesus Christ our Lord.

REINHOLD NIEBUHR, TWENTIETH CENTURY

Father, forgive

The hatred which divides nation from nation,
race from race, class from class,
Father, forgive.
The covetous desires of men and nations
to possess what is not their own,
Father, forgive.
The greed which exploits the labours of men,
and lays waste the earth,
Father, forgive.
Our envy of the welfare and happiness of others,
Father, forgive.
Our indifference to the plight of the homeless
and the refugee,
Father, forgive.
The lust which uses for ignoble ends
the bodies of men and women,
Father, forgive.
The pride which leads to trust in ourselves,
and not in God,
Father, forgive.

COVENTRY CATHEDRAL PRAYER, 1964

PART TWO

PRAYERS FOR EVERY OCCASION

THE GREATNESS OF GOD

It is good to sing praise to our God;
it is pleasant and right to praise him.

<small>FROM THE BOOK OF PSALMS, CHAPTER 147</small>

Worship in heaven

Y ou are worthy, our Lord and God, to receive glory and honour
and power, for you created all things, and by your will they
existed and were created.

<small>FROM THE BOOK OF REVELATION, CHAPTER 4</small>

Ruler of the world

O Lord, ruler of the world,
even while the earth was without form you were King
and you will still reign when all things are brought to an end.
You are supreme and you will never be equalled.
You are power and might:
there is neither beginning nor end in you.

<small>JEWISH PRAYER</small>

St Francis' hymn of praise

Holy, holy, holy is the Lord God Almighty,
    who is, who was and who is to come.
Let us praise and glorify him for ever.
You are worthy, Lord our God,
    to receive praise and glory,
    honour and blessing.
Let us praise and glorify him for ever.
Worthy is the Lamb that was slain to receive
    divine power, wisdom and strength,
    honour, glory and blessing.
Let us praise and glorify him for ever.
Bless the Lord all you works of the Lord.
Let us praise and glorify him for ever.
Praise our God all you his servants,
    honour him, you who fear God, small and great.
Let us praise and glorify him for ever.
Let heaven and earth praise your glory:
    all creatures in heaven, on earth and under the earth,
    the sea and everything in it.
Let us praise and glorify him for ever.

St Francis of Assisi, thirteenth century

The holy trinity

O Father, my hope
O Son, my refuge
O Holy Spirit, my protection
Holy Trinity, glory to thee.

<small>St Joannikios, from the service of Compline, Eastern Orthodox Church</small>

God three in one

Glory to the father, who has woven garments of glory for the resurrection; worship to the Son, who was clothed in them at his rising; thanksgiving to the Spirit, who keeps them for all the saints; one nature in three, to him be praise.

<small>Syrian Orthodox Church</small>

Thou art the creator

I believe, O Lord and God of the peoples,
that thou art the creator of the high heavens,
that thou art the creator of the skies above,
that thou art the creator of the oceans below.

I believe, O Lord and God of the peoples,
that thou art he who created my soul and set its warp,
who created my body from dust and from ashes,
who gave to my body breath, and to my soul its possession.

FROM THE CARMINA GADELICA

Let us praise God

Let us, with a gladsome mind
praise the Lord, for he is kind;
for his mercies shall endure,
ever faithful, ever sure.

JOHN MILTON, SEVENTEENTH CENTURY

SEEKING THE FACE OF GOD

Y ou will seek me and find me when you seek me with all your
heart.

FROM THE BOOK OF JEREMIAH, CHAPTER 29

Amongst the rush and noise

In the rush and noise of life, as you have intervals, step within
yourselves and be still. Wait upon God and feel his good presence;
this will carry you through your day's business.

WILLIAM PENN, SEVENTEENTH CENTURY

The boy Samuel's prayer

Speak, Lord, your servant is listening.

FROM THE FIRST BOOK OF SAMUEL, CHAPTER 3

A *cloud of unknowing*

Do not give up…
When you first begin, you find only darkness
and as it were a cloud of unknowing.
You don't know what this means
except that in your will you feel
a simple, steadfast intention
reaching out towards God…
Reconcile yourself to wait in this darkness
as long as is necessary,
but still go on longing after him whom you love.

FROM *THE CLOUD OF UNKNOWING*, FOURTEENTH CENTURY

The psalmist's cry for help

My God, my God, why have you forsaken me?
Why are you so far from helping me,
   from the words of my groaning?
O my God, I cry by day, but you do not answer;
   and by night, but find no rest...
Yet it was you who took me from the womb;
   you kept me safe on my mother's breast.
On you I was cast from my birth,
   and since my mother bore me you have been my God.
Do not be far from me,
   for trouble is near
   and there is no one to help.

FROM THE BOOK OF PSALMS, CHAPTER 22

Sufficient for me

God of your goodness, give me yourself,
for you are sufficient for me…
If I were to ask anything less
I should always be in want,
for in you alone do I have all.

JULIAN OF NORWICH, FOURTEENTH CENTURY

Wherever I go

There is no place where God is not,
wherever I go, there God is.
Now and always he upholds me with his power
and keeps me safe in his love.

AUTHOR UNKNOWN

A hunger for God

O God, the living God, who has put your own eternity in our hearts, and has made us to hunger and thirst after you: satisfy, we pray you, the instincts which you have implanted in us that we may find you in life, and life in you; through Jesus Christ our Lord.

AUTHOR UNKNOWN

LISTENING

Be still, and know that I am God.

FROM THE BOOK OF PSALMS, CHAPTER 46

So still

O make my heart so still, so still,
when I am deep in prayer,
that I might hear the white mist-wreaths
losing themselves in air!

UTSONOMYA SAN, JAPAN

A call to meditation

Come now, little man,
turn aside for a while
from your daily employment,
escape for a moment
from the tumult of your thoughts.
Put aside your weighty cares,
let your burdensome distractions wait,
free yourself awhile for God
and rest awhile in him.
Enter the inner chamber of your soul,
shut out everything except God
and that which can help you in seeking him,
and when you have shut the door, seek him.
Now, my whole heart, say to God,
'I seek your face, Lord,
it is your face I seek.'

ST ANSELM OF CANTERBURY, ELEVENTH CENTURY

Silence

All is silent.
In the still and soundless air,
I fervently bow
to my almighty God.

HSIEH PING-HSIN, CHINA

A time for silence

O Lord,
the Scripture says,
'There is a time for silence
and a time for speech.'
Saviour, teach me
the silence of humility,
the silence of wisdom,
the silence of love,
the silence of perfection,
the silence that speaks without words,
the silence of faith.
Lord teach me to silence my own heart
that I may listen to the gentle movement
of the Holy Spirit within me
and sense the depths which are of God.

AUTHOR UNKNOWN, SIXTEENTH CENTURY

FINDING FORGIVENESS

If we confess our sins, he who is faithful and just, will forgive us our sins and cleanse us from all unrighteousness.

From the first letter of John, chapter 1

The Jesus prayer

In the Eastern Orthodox Church this prayer is said over and over again as a way into prayer.

Lord Jesus Christ,
Son of God,
have mercy on me,
a sinner.

The general confession

Almighty and most merciful Father,
    we have erred, and strayed from thy ways
    like lost sheep.
We have followed too much the devices and desires
    of our own hearts.
We have offended against thy holy laws.
We have left undone those things
    which we ought to have done;
    and we have done those things
    which we ought not to have done;
    and there is no health in us.
But thou, O Lord, have mercy upon us, miserable
    offenders.
Spare thou them, O God, which confess their faults.
Restore thou them that are penitent;
    according to thy promises declared unto mankind
    in Christ Jesu our Lord.
And grant, O most merciful Father, for his sake;
    that we may hereafter live a godly, righteous,
    and sober life, to the glory of thy holy Name.

FROM THE BOOK OF COMMON PRAYER

Forgive us our sins

Forgive them all, O Lord:
our sins of omission and our sins of commission;
the sins of our youth and the sins of our riper years;
the sins of our souls and the sins of our bodies;
our secret and our more open sins;
our sins of ignorance and surprise,
and our more deliberate and presumptuous sins;
the sins we have done to please ourselves,
and the sins we have done to please others;
the sins we know and remember,
and the sins we have forgotten;
the sins we have striven to hide from others,
and the sins by which we have made others offend;
forgive them, O Lord, forgive them all for his sake,
who died for our sins and rose for our justification,
and now stands at thy right hand
to make intercession for us,
Jesus Christ our Lord.

JOHN WESLEY, EIGHTEENTH CENTURY

Like a child

Lord, I have given up my pride
and turned away from my arrogance.
I am not concerned with great matters
or with subjects too difficult for me.
Instead, I am content and at peace.
As a child lies quietly in its mother's arms,
so my heart is quiet within me.

FROM THE BOOK OF PSALMS, CHAPTER 131

Rock of ages

Rock of ages, cleft for me,
let me hide myself in thee:
let the water and the blood
from thy riven side which flowed,
be of sin the double cure –
cleanse me from its guilt and power.

AUGUSTUS TOPLADY, EIGHTEENTH CENTURY

Offering ourselves to God

I heard the voice of the Lord saying,
'Whom shall I send, and who will go for us?'
Then said I, 'Here am I; send me.'

<small>FROM THE BOOK OF ISAIAH, CHAPTER 6</small>

To thee I live

To thee, O Jesu, I direct my eyes;
to thee my hands, to thee my humble knees;
to thee my heart shall offer sacrifice;
to thee my thoughts, who my thoughts only sees;
to thee my self – my self and all I give;
to thee I die;
to thee I only live.

<small>ATTRIBUTED TO SIR WALTER RALEIGH, SIXTEENTH CENTURY</small>

God's word in our lives

Give us grace, O Lord, not only to hear thy word with our ears,
but also to receive it into our hearts and to show it forth in
our lives; for the glory of thy great name.

<small>AUTHOR UNKNOWN</small>

Given to God

Lord Jesus,
I give thee my hands to do thy work.
I give thee my feet to go thy way.
I give thee my eyes to see as thou seest.
I give thee my tongue to speak thy words.
I give thee my mind that thou mayest think in me.
I give thee my spirit that thou mayest pray in me.
Above all, I give thee my heart
   that thou mayest love in me
   thy Father, and all mankind.
I give thee my whole self
   that thou mayest grow in me,
   so that it is thee, Lord Jesus,
   who lives and works and prays in me.
I hand over to thy care, Lord,
   my soul and body,
   my prayers and my hopes,
   my health and my work,
   my life and my death,
   my parents and my family,
   my friends and my neighbours,
   my country and all men,
   today and always.

LANCELOT ANDREWES, SIXTEENTH CENTURY

My *whole life*

I am giving thee worship
with my whole life,

I am giving thee assent
with my whole power,

I am giving thee praise
with my whole tongue,

I am giving thee honour
with my whole utterance,

I am giving thee reverence
with my whole understanding,

I am giving thee offering
with my whole thought,

I am giving thee praise
with my whole fervour,

I am giving thee humility
in the blood of the Lamb.

I am giving thee love
with my whole devotion,

I am giving thee kneeling
with my whole desire,

I am giving thee love
with my whole heart,

I am giving thee affection
with my whole sense;

I am giving thee my existence
with my whole mind,

I am giving thee my soul,
O God of all gods.

ANCIENT SCOTTISH PRAYER

Full contentment

Be thou a light unto my eyes,
music to mine ears,
sweetness to my taste,
and full contentment to my heart.
Be thou my sunshine in the day,
my food at table,
my repose in the night,
my clothing in nakedness,
and my succour in all necessities.
Lord Jesu, I give thee my body, my soul,
my substance, my fame, my friends,
my liberty and my life.
Dispose of me and all that is mine
as it may seem best to thee
and to the glory of thy blessed name.

JOHN COSIN, SEVENTEENTH CENTURY

Wanting what God wants

Lord, thou knowest what I want,
if it be thy will that I have it,
and if it be not thy will,
good Lord, do not be displeased,
for I want nothing which you do not want.

JULIAN OF NORWICH, FOURTEENTH CENTURY

THANKS AND PRAISE

Praise the Lord, my soul!
All my being, praise his holy name!

FROM THE BOOK OF PSALMS, CHAPTER 103

Glory to God

Glory to God,
Oh, the depth of the riches of the wisdom
and knowledge of God!
How unsearchable his judgments,
and his paths beyond tracing out!
Who has known the mind of the Lord?
Or who has been his counsellor?
Who has ever given to God,
that God should repay him?
For from him and through him and to him are all things.
To him be the glory for ever!

FROM THE LETTER TO THE ROMANS, CHAPTER 11

The general thanksgiving

Almighty God, Father of all mercies,
    we thine unworthy servants
    do give thee most humble and hearty thanks
    for all thy goodness and loving-kindness to us,
    and to all men.
We bless thee for our creation, preservation,
    and all the blessings of this life;
    but above all, for thine inestimable love
    in the redemption of the world
    by our Lord Jesus Christ;
    for the means of grace, and for the hope of glory.
And, we beseech thee,
    give us that due sense of all thy mercies,
    that our hearts may be unfeignedly thankful,
    and that we show forth thy praise,
    not only with our lips, but in our lives;
    by giving up ourselves to thy service,
    and by walking before thee in holiness
    and righteousness all our days;
    through Jesus Christ our Lord, to whom with thee
    and the Holy Ghost be all honour and glory,
    world without end.

FROM THE BOOK OF COMMON PRAYER

In every corner sing

Let all the world in every corner sing,
'My God and King!'
The heavens are not too high,
his praise may thither fly.
The earth is not too low,
his praises there may grow.
The church with psalms must shout,
no door can keep them out.
But, above all, the heart
must bear the longest part.
Let all the world in every corner sing,
'My God and King!'

GEORGE HERBERT, SEVENTEENTH CENTURY

Now thank we all our God

Now thank we all our God,
with heart and hands and voices,
who wondrous things hath done,
in whom his world rejoices;
who from our mothers' arms
hath blessed us on our way
with countless gifts of love,
and still is ours today.

MARTIN RINCKART, SEVENTEENTH CENTURY

The pleasure of the senses

I thank you, O God, for the pleasures you have given me
through my senses; for the glory of thunder, for the mystery
of music, the singing of birds and the laughter of children.
I thank you for the delights of colour, the awe of the sunset,
the wild roses in the hedgerows, the smile of friendship.
I thank you for the sweetness of flowers and the scent of hay.
Truly, O Lord, the earth is full of your riches!

AFTER EDWARD KING, NINETEENTH CENTURY

A child's prayer

Thank God for rain
and the beautiful rainbow colours
and thank God for letting children
splash in the puddles.

AUTHOR UNKNOWN

ALL KINDS OF REQUESTS

Don't worry about anything, but in all your prayers ask God for what you need, always asking him with a thankful heart.

FROM THE LETTER TO THE PHILIPPIANS, CHAPTER 4

Prayers and responses

The Lord be with you.
And with thy spirit.
Let us pray.

Lord, have mercy upon us.
Christ, have mercy upon us.
Lord, have mercy upon us.

Oh Lord, hear our prayer.
And let our cry come unto thee.

FROM THE BOOK OF COMMON PRAYER

FOR OURSELVES

Only a spark

I am only a spark;
make me a fire.
I am only a string;
make me a lyre.
I am only a drop;
make me a fountain.
I am only an ant hill;
make me a mountain.
I am only a feather;
make me a wing.
I am only a rag;
make me a king!

PRAYER FROM MEXICO

Perfect love casts out fear

O God, it is so hard for us not to be anxious.
We worry about work and money,
about food and health,
about weather and crops,
about war and politics,
about loving and being loved.
Show us how perfect love casts out fear.

MONICA FURLONG, TWENTIETH CENTURY

Give us dreams

God give us rain when we expect sun.
Give us music when we expect trouble.
Give us tears when we expect breakfast.
Give us dreams when we expect a storm.
Give us a stray dog when we expect congratulations.
God play with us, turn us sideways and around.

MICHAEL LEUNIG, TWENTIETH CENTURY

For our hearts

Grant unto us your servants
to our God – a heart of flame
to our fellow men – a heart of love
to ourselves – a heart of steel.

ST AUGUSTINE OF HIPPO, FIFTH CENTURY

A guiding star

My dearest Lord,
be thou a bright flame before me,
be thou a guiding star above me,
be thou a smooth path beneath me,
be thou a kindly shepherd behind me,
today and for evermore.

ST COLUMBA OF IONA, SIXTH CENTURY

FOR FRIENDS AND NEIGHBOURS

Brotherly love

It is your will that we not only call you father, but that all of us together call you *our* Father, and thus offer our prayers with one accord for all. Grant us, therefore, brotherly love and unity, that we may know and think of one another as true brothers and sisters, and pray to you, our own common Father, for all people and for every person, even as one child prays for another to its father.

Let no one among us seek his own good or forget before you the good of others; but, all hatred, envy, and dissension laid aside, may we love one another as good and true children of God, and thus say with one accord not 'my Father', but '*our* Father'.

MARTIN LUTHER, SIXTEENTH CENTURY

For a friend

Christ who first gave thee for a friend to me,
Christ keep thee well, where'er thou art, for me.
Earth's self shall go and the swift wheel of heaven
perish and pass, before our love shall cease.
Do but remember me, as I do thee,
and God, who brought us on this earth together,
bring us together in his house of heaven.

Rabanus Maurus, ninth century

Broken friendships

Dear God, lover of us all, do not let me go down into the grave with old broken friendships unresolved. Give to us and to all with whom we have shared our lives and deepest selves along the way, the courage not only to express anger when we feel let down, but your more generous love which always seeks to reconcile and so to build a more enduring love between those we have held dear as friends.

Kathy Keay, twentieth century

For our neighbours

Lord, you taught us that all who come our way are our neighbours. But hear our prayer for those with whom we come in daily contact because they live close to us. Help us to be good neighbours to them. Give us the grace to overlook petty annoyances and to build on all that is positive in our relationship, that we may love them as we love ourselves, with genuine forbearance and kindness. For Jesus' sake.

AUTHOR UNKNOWN

Love one another

Almighty God and most merciful Father, who has given us a new commandment that we should love one another, give us also grace that we may fulfil it. Make us gentle, courteous and forbearing. Direct our lives so that we may look to the good of the other in word and deed. And hallow all our friendships by the blessing of your Spirit, for his sake who loved us and gave himself for us, Jesus Christ our Lord.

BROOKE FOSS WESTCOTT, NINETEENTH CENTURY

FOR HOME AND FAMILY

Around our table

Father of all mankind, make the roof of my house wide enough for all opinions, oil the door of my house so it opens easily to friend and stranger and set such a table in my house that my whole family may speak kindly and freely around it.

Prayer from Hawaii

A blessing on this house

God bless the house
from site to stay,
from beam to wall,
from end to end,
from ridge to basement,
from balk to roof-tree,
from found to summit,
found and summit.

Celtic prayer

All poor men abroad

When you sit happy in your own fair house,
remember all poor men that are abroad,
eternal dwelling in the house of God.

Alcuin of York, eighth century

Our family

L ord, behold our family here assembled. We thank thee for this place in which we dwell; for the love that unites us; for the peace accorded us this day; for the hope which we expect the morrow; for the health, the work, the food, and the bright skies, that make our life delightful; for our friends in all parts of the earth and our friendly helpers in this foreign isle. Let peace abound in our small community. Purge out of every heart the lurking grudge. Give us grace and strength to forbear and to persevere… Give us courage, gaiety and the quiet mind.

ROBERT LOUIS STEVENSON, NINETEENTH CENTURY

Merry meeting

Pray for me as I will for thee,
that we may merrily meet in heaven.

THOMAS MORE, SIXTEENTH CENTURY

In absence

Holy Father, in your mercy,
hear our earnest prayer,
keep our loved ones, now far distant,
'neath your care.

When in sorrow, when in danger,
when in loneliness,
in your love look down and comfort
their distress.

May the joy of your salvation
be their strength and stay;
may they love and may they praise you
day by day.

ISABEL STEVENSON, NINETEENTH CENTURY

On parting

The Lord watch between me and thee
when we are absent one from another.

FROM THE BOOK OF GENESIS, CHAPTER 31

THE WORLD OF WORK

Daily labour

Forth in your name, O Lord, I go,
my daily labour to pursue,
you, only you, resolved to know
in all I think, or speak or do.

The task your wisdom has assigned
O let me cheerfully fulfil,
in all my works your presence find,
and prove your good and perfect will.

CHARLES WESLEY, EIGHTEENTH CENTURY

As for thee

Teach me, my God and King,
in all things thee to see,
and what I do in anything
to do it as for thee.

GEORGE HERBERT, SEVENTEENTH CENTURY

Our work

OLord, renew our spirits and draw our hearts unto yourself, that our work may not be a burden, but a delight; and give us such a mighty love to you as may sweeten our obedience. O let us not serve you with the spirit of bondage as slaves, but with cheerfulness and gladness, delighting in you and rejoicing in your work.

BENJAMIN JENKS, EIGHTEENTH CENTURY

Contentment

Lord, in times of poverty make me perfectly content,
and in times of wealth make me generous and liberal.

JOHN EDDISON

All our gifts

O Lord our God,
give us by your Holy Spirit
a willing heart and a ready hand
to use all your gifts
to your praise and glory;
through Jesus Christ our Lord.

THOMAS CRANMER, SIXTEENTH CENTURY

FOR OUR BEAUTIFUL WORLD

All this beauty

O God, we thank you for this earth, our home; for the wide sky and the blessed sun, for the salt sea and the running water, for the everlasting hills and the never-resting winds, for trees and the common grass underfoot. We thank you for our senses by which we hear the songs of birds, and see the splendour of the summer fields, and taste of the autumn fruits, and rejoice in the feel of the snow, and smell the breath of the spring. Grant us a heart wide open to all this beauty; and save our souls from being so blind that we pass unseeing when even the common thornbush is aflame with your glory, O God our creator, who lives and reigns for ever and ever.

WALTER RAUSCHENBUSCH, TWENTIETH CENTURY

Eyes to see

Lord, purge our eyes to see
within the seed a tree,
within the glowing egg a bird,
within the shroud a butterfly.
Till, taught by such we see
beyond all creatures, thee
and hearken to thy tender word
and hear its 'Fear not; it is I.'

CHRISTINA ROSSETTI, NINETEENTH CENTURY

Share the vision

As the hand is made for holding
and the eye for seeing,
you have fashioned me, O Lord, for joy.
Share with me the vision
to find that joy everywhere:
in the wild violet's beauty,
in the lark's melody,
in the face of a steadfast man,
in a child's smile,
in a mother's love,
in the purity of Jesus.

CELTIC PRAYER

A blessing

Bless this year for us, O our God, and bless every species of its fruits for our benefit. Bestow a blessing upon the face of the earth, and satisfy us with your goodness. O bless our years, and make them good years; for your honour and glory.

POLISH JEWISH PRAYER

For the animals

We pray, Lord, for the humble beasts who with us bear
the burden and heat of the day, giving their lives for
the well-being of their countries; and for the wild creatures,
whom you have made wise, strong and beautiful; we ask for
them your great tenderness of heart, for you have promised
to save both man and beast, and great is your loving-kindness,
O Saviour of the world.

RUSSIAN PRAYER

For animals who suffer

Hear our humble prayer, O God, for our friends the animals,
especially for animals who are suffering; for any that are
hunted or lost or deserted or frightened or hungry; for all that
must be put to death. We entreat for them all thy mercy and
pity and for those who deal with them we ask a heart of
compassion, gentle hands and kindly words. Make us ourselves
to be true friends to animals and so to share the blessing of the
merciful.

ALBERT SCHWEITZER, TWENTIETH CENTURY

Bless our land

Bless our beautiful land, O Lord,
with its wonderful variety of people,
of races, cultures and languages.
May we be a nation
of laughter and joy,
of justice and reconciliation,
of peace and unity,
of compassion, caring and sharing.
We pray this prayer for a true patriotism,
in the powerful name of Jesus our Lord.

DESMOND TUTU, TWENTIETH CENTURY

Pour forth,
O Christ,
your love
upon this land
today.

AUTHOR UNKNOWN

FOR PEACE

Turn our hearts

To you, O Son of God, Lord Jesus Christ,
as you pray to the eternal Father,
we pray, make us one in him.
Lighten our personal distress
and that of our society.
Receive us into the fellowship
of those who believe.
Turn our hearts, O Christ,
to everlasting truth
and healing harmony.

PHILIP MELANCHTHON, SIXTEENTH CENTURY

To do our part

God our Father, Creator of the world,
please help us to love one another.
Make nations friendly with other nations;
make all of us love one another like brothers and sisters.
Help us to do our part to bring peace in the world
and happiness to all people.

PRAYER FROM JAPAN

This is my hope

This is my song, O God of all nations,
a song of peace for lands afar, and mine.
This is my hope, the country where my heart is.
this is my hope, my dream, and my shrine.
But other hearts in other lands are beating
with hopes and dreams that are the same as mine.
My country's skies are bluer than the ocean,
the sunlight beams on clover leafs and pine;
but other lands have sunlight too, and clover,
and other skies are just as blue as mine.
O hear my prayer, thou God of all the nations,
a prayer of peace for other lands and mine.

AUTHOR UNKNOWN

FOR THOSE WHO SUFFER

You are mine

Oh God, you have said:
Do not be afraid – I will save you.
I have called you by name – you are mine.
When you pass through deep waters,
I will be with you;
your troubles will not overwhelm you.
Help me to hear you say these words to me.

<small>BASED ON THE BOOK OF ISAIAH, CHAPTER 43</small>

God is unchanging

Let nothing disturb you, nothing alarm you:
while all things fade away
God is unchanging.
Be patient
and you will gain everything:
for with God in your heart
nothing is lacking,
God meets your every need.

<small>ST TERESA OF AVILA, SIXTEENTH CENTURY</small>

Cares and sorrows

Heavenly Father,
we bring to you in prayer
people who are suffering in mind or spirit.

We remember especially those facing long and incurable illness;
those cast down by the cares and sorrows of daily life;
those who have lost their faith and for whom the future is dark.

In your mercy maintain their courage,
lift their burdens and renew their faith,
that they may find in you their strength,
their comfort and their peace,
for our Saviour's sake.

FRANK COLQUHOUN, TWENTIETH CENTURY

Preserve us from fear

Most loving Father, preserve us from faithless fears and worldly anxieties and grant that no clouds of this mortal life may hide from us the light of that love which is immortal and which you have manifested unto us in your Son, Jesus Christ our Lord.

WILLIAM BRIGHT, NINETEENTH CENTURY

The fruits of suffering

If I had not suffered
I would not have known the love of God.
If many people had not suffered
God's love would not have been passed on.
If Jesus had not suffered
God's love would not have been made visible.

MIZUNO GENZO, JAPAN

FOR THOSE WHO GRIEVE

My heart is dead

Ah Lord, my prayers are dead,
my affections dead
and my heart is dead;
but you are a living God
and I bear myself upon you.

<small>WILLIAM BRIDGE, SEVENTEENTH CENTURY</small>

Abide with me

Abide with me;
fast falls the eventide;
the darkness deepens;
Lord with me abide!
When other helpers fail,
and comforts flee,
Help of the helpless,
O abide with me.

<small>HENRY FRANCIS LYTE, NINETEENTH CENTURY</small>

For those in pain

Grant, O Lord,
to all those who are bearing pain,
thy spirit of healing,
thy spirit of life,
thy spirit of peace and hope,
of courage and endurance.
Cast out from them
the spirit of anxiety and fear;
grant them perfect confidence and trust in thee,
that in thy light they may see light,
through Jesus Christ our Lord.

AUTHOR UNKNOWN

FOR THE OPPRESSED

De profundis

From the depths of my despair
I call to you, Lord.
Hear my cry, O Lord;
listen to my call for help!

FROM THE BOOK OF PSALMS, CHAPTER 130

A place of tears

Eternal God,
we confess to you our sinfulness.
You made the world a paradise
but we have turned our lands into
places of tears and unhappiness.
People are fighting with each other
race against race.
The holocaust of chauvinism sweeps through countries,
devouring humanity, terrorizing us into submission.

Liberating One,
free us from all bondage
so that our faith in you will make us free
to create with courage
a new world – new societies.

PRAYER FROM SRI LANKA

Strengthen us

Strengthen us, O God, to relieve the oppressed,
to hear the groans of poor prisoners,
to reform the abuses of all professions;
that many be made not poor to make a few rich;
for Jesus Christ's sake.

OLIVER CROMWELL, SEVENTEENTH CENTURY

Homelessness

Have mercy, O God, on all who are sorrowful,
those who weep and those in exile.
Have pity on the persecuted and the homeless
who are without hope;
those who are scattered in remote corners of this world;
those who are in prison and ruled by tyrants.
Have mercy on them as is written in your holy law,
where your compassion is exalted!

JEWISH PRAYER

Against hunger

O God our Father, in the name of him who gave bread to the hungry we remember all who through our human ignorance, selfishness and sin are condemned to live in want; and we pray that all endeavours for the overcoming of world poverty and hunger may be so prospered that there may be found food sufficient for all; through Jesus Christ our Lord.

Christian Aid prayer

For equity

O God of integrity,
of the fair measure and the just weight,
may we show forth your holiness
not only in our worship
but in our business deals:
that the world may be freed
from its slavery to unjust trade,
through Jesus Christ

Janet Morley, twentieth century

TIMES AND SEASONS

MORNING

Morning light

My Father, for another night of quiet sleep and rest,
for all the joy of morning light, your holy name be blest.

HENRY WILLIAMS BAKER, NINETEENTH CENTURY

Every minute

Through every minute of this day,
be with me, Lord!
Through every day of all this week,
be with me, Lord!
Through every week of all this year,
be with me, Lord!
Through all the years of all this life,
be with me, Lord!
So shall the days and weeks and years
be threaded on a golden cord.
And all draw on with sweet accord
unto thy fullness, Lord,
that so, when time is past,
by grace I may, at last,
be with thee, Lord.

JOHN OXENHAM, TWENTIETH CENTURY

EVENING

Stay with us, Lord;
the day is almost over and it is getting dark.

BASED ON THE GOSPEL OF LUKE, CHAPTER 24

Before sleep

Ere thou sleepest, gently lay
every troubled thought away.
Put off worry and distress
as thou puttest off thy dress.
Drop thy worry and thy care
in the quiet arms of prayer.
Lord, thou knowest how I live;
all I've done amiss, forgive;
all the good I've tried to do
hallow, bless, and carry through.
All I love in safety keep,
while, in thee, I fall asleep.

AUTHOR UNKNOWN

While we are asleep

Save us Lord, while we are awake;
guard us while we are asleep;
that awake we may watch with Christ,
and asleep may rest in his peace.

The church unsleeping

The day thou gavest, Lord, is ended,
the darkness falls at thy behest;
to thee our morning hymns ascended,
thy praise shall sanctify our rest.

We thank thee that thy Church unsleeping,
while earth rolls onward into light,
through all the world her watch is keeping,
and rests not now by day or night.

As o'er each continent and island
the dawn leads on another day,
the voice of prayer is never silent,
nor dies the strain of praise away.

The sun that bids us rest is waking
our brethren 'neath the western sky,
and hour by hour fresh lips are making
thy wondrous doings heard on high.

So be it, Lord; thy throne shall never,
like earth's proud empires, pass away;
thy Kingdom stands, and grows for ever,
till all thy creatures own thy sway.

JOHN ELLERTON, NINETEENTH CENTURY

SUNDAY

Rejoice

This is the day that the Lord has made;
let us rejoice and be glad in it.

<small>FROM THE BOOK OF PSALMS, CHAPTER 118</small>

The Lord is risen

The Lord is risen indeed!

<small>FROM THE GOSPEL OF LUKE, CHAPTER 24</small>

Morning prayer

O Lord, our heavenly Father,
almighty and everlasting God,
who hast safely brought us to the beginning of this day,
defend us in the same with thy mighty power,
and grant that this day we fall into no sin,
neither run into any kind of danger,
but that all our doings may be ordered by
     thy governance,
to do always that is righteous in thy sight,
through Jesus Christ our Lord.

<small>FROM THE BOOK OF COMMON PRAYER</small>

HOLY COMMUNION OR EUCHARIST

Spiritual food

O Lord, thank you for bread, your body, given for me;
thank you for wine, your blood, poured out for me.
May this spiritual food be my strength and my joy,
until I come to you again.

AUTHOR UNKNOWN

Look to Jesus

Look, Father, look on his anointed face,
and only look on us as found in him;
look not on our misusings of thy grace,
our prayer so languid and our faith so dim.
For, lo, between our sins and their reward
we set the passion of thy Son our Lord.

WILLIAM BRIGHT, NINETEENTH CENTURY

To live and work

Almighty God,
we thank you for feeding us
with the body and blood of your Son, Jesus Christ.
Through him we offer you our souls and bodies
to be a living sacrifice.
Send us out in the power of your Spirit
to live and work
to your praise and glory.

FROM THE ALTERNATIVE SERVICE BOOK

Ready for service

Strengthen for service, Lord, the hands that have taken holy
things; may the ears which have heard your word be deaf to
clamour and dispute; may the tongues which have sung your praise
be free from deceit; may the eyes which have seen the tokens of
your love shine with the light of hope; and may the bodies which
have been fed with your body be refreshed with the fullness of your
life; glory to you for ever.

FROM THE SYRIAC LITURGY OF MALABAR

ADVENT

The armour of light

Almighty God,
give us grace to cast away the works of darkness
and to put on the armour of light,
now in the time of this mortal life,
in which your son Jesus Christ came to us
in great humility;
so that on the last day,
when he shall come again in his glorious majesty
to judge the living and the dead,
we may rise to the life immortal,
through him who is alive and reigns with you
and the Holy Spirit, now and ever.

FROM THE ALTERNATIVE SERVICE BOOK

Open hearts

At Advent we should try the key to our heart's door. It may
have gathered rust. If so, this is the time to oil it, in order
that the heart's door may open more easily when the Lord
Jesus wants to enter at Christmas time!

Lord, oil the hinges of our hearts' doors that they may
swing gently and easily to welcome your coming.

PRAYER OF A NEW GUINEA CHRISTIAN

CHRISTMAS

Child of glory

The child of glory,
the child of Mary,
born in the stable
the King of all,
who came to the wilderness
and in our stead suffered;
happy they are counted
who to him are near.

CELTIC PRAYER

Kept for thee

Ah, dearest Jesus,
holy child,
make thee a bed,
soft, undefiled,
within my heart,
that it may be
a quiet chamber
kept for thee.

MARTIN LUTHER, SIXTEENTH CENTURY

Glory to the new-born King

Hark! the herald-angels sing
glory to the new-born King,
peace on earth and mercy mild,
God and sinners reconciled.
Joyful, all ye nations, rise,
join the triumph of the skies;
with the angelic host proclaim,
'Christ is born in Bethlehem.'
Hark! the herald-angels sing
glory to the new-born King.

<small>CHARLES WESLEY, EIGHTEENTH CENTURY</small>

Christmas night

O God who has made this most hallowed night resplendent
with the glory of the true Light; grant that we who have
known the mysteries of that Light on earth, may enter into the
fullness of his joys in heaven.

<small>FROM THE WESTERN RITE FOR CHRISTMAS MIDNIGHT</small>

LENT

To keep the fast

O Lord, who for our sake didst fast forty days and forty nights; give us grace to use such abstinence, that, our flesh being subdued to the Spirit, we may ever obey thy godly motions in righteousness, and true holiness, to thy honour and glory, who livest and reignest with the Father and the Holy Ghost, one God, world without end.

FROM THE BOOK OF COMMON PRAYER

To grow in grace

And now we give you thanks because through him you have given us the spirit of discipline, that we may triumph over evil and grow in grace.

FROM THE ALTERNATIVE SERVICE BOOK

MOTHERING SUNDAY

Mother's love

Thank you, Lord, for our mothers. We remember today their loving care, and their ceaseless love for us. May we show them by our gifts, our words and our actions that we love them and care about them too.

AUTHOR UNKNOWN

Our mother church

Father, we thank you for the family of the church. Thank you for those who are true mothers within our Christian family. May they know your blessing and strength as they care for others.

AUTHOR UNKNOWN

PALM SUNDAY

Hosanna! Blessed is the one who comes in the name of the Lord.

FROM THE GOSPEL OF MARK, CHAPTER 11

The humble king

Shout for joy, you people of Jerusalem! Look, your king is coming to you! He comes triumphant and victorious, but humble and riding on a donkey.

FROM THE BOOK OF ZECHARIAH, CHAPTER 9

Give praise to Christ

Let the mountains and all the hills
break out into great rejoicing at the mercy of God,
and let the trees of the forest clap their hands.
Give praise to Christ, all nations,
magnify him, all peoples, crying:
'Glory to thy power, O Lord.'

Seated in heaven upon thy throne
and on earth upon a foal, O Christ our God,
thou hast accepted the praise of the angels
and the songs of the children who cried out to thee:
'Blessed art thou that comest to call back Adam.'

EASTERN ORTHODOX CHURCH

GOOD FRIDAY

The just for the unjust

Christ died for sins once for all,
the just for the unjust,
to bring us to God:
he was put to death in the body,
but made alive by the Spirit;
he has gone up on high,
and is at God's right hand,
ruling over angels
and the powers of heaven.

BASED ON THE FIRST LETTER OF PETER, CHAPTER 3

O sacred head

O sacred head! sore wounded,
with grief and shame bowed down,
now scornfully surrounded
with thorns, thy only crown!
How pale art thou with anguish,
with sore abuse and scorn!
How does that visage languish,
which once was bright as morn!

ST BERNARD OF CLAIRVAUX, TWELFTH CENTURY

EASTER

Christ has risen

Christ has risen from the dead,
by death defeating death,
and those buried in the grave
he has brought back to life.

THE EASTER TROPARION FROM THE ORTHODOX CHURCH

The battle is done

The strife is o'er, the battle done;
Now is the victor's triumph won,
O let the song of praise be sung:
Alleluia!

LATIN HYMN, EIGHTEENTH CENTURY

He will come again

Christ has died,
Christ is risen,
Christ will come again.

FROM THE BOOK OF COMMON PRAYER

WHITSUN OR PENTECOST

Celestial fire

Come, Holy Ghost, our souls inspire,
and lighten with celestial fire:
thou the anointing Spirit art,
who does thy sevenfold gifts impart.

JOHN COSIN, SEVENTEENTH CENTURY

The gift of grace

O God,
you have graciously brought us to this hour,
the time when you poured out your Holy Spirit
in tongues of fire upon your apostles,
filling them with the gift of your grace;
so, most wonderful Lord,
may we too receive this blessing;
and as we seek to praise you, merciful God,
in psalms and hymns and spiritual songs,
may we share in your eternal kingdom.
For your name is worthy of all honour and majesty
and you are to be glorified in hymns of blessing,
Father, Son and Holy Spirit,
now and for ever, to the ages of ages.

EASTERN ORTHODOX CHURCH

HARVEST

Bread from the earth

Blessed art thou, O Lord our God,
King of the universe,
who bringest forth bread from the earth.

JEWISH BLESSING

All good gifts

We plough the fields, and scatter
the good seed on the land,
but it is fed and watered
by God's almighty hand:
he sends the snow in winter,
the warmth to swell the grain,
the breezes, and the sunshine,
and soft, refreshing rain.

All good gifts around us
are sent from heaven above;
then thank the Lord, O thank the Lord,
for all his love.

MATTHIAS CLAUDIUS, EIGHTEENTH CENTURY

FAMILY OCCASIONS

A NEW BABY

Wonder and joy

God our Father, maker of all that is living, we praise you for the wonder and joy of creation. We thank you from our hearts for the life of this child, for a safe delivery, and for the privilege of parenthood. Accept our thanks and praise through Jesus Christ our Lord.

FROM THE ALTERNATIVE SERVICE BOOK

Welcome baby

Welcome baby, special person,
welcome to our world
like a leafbud, tightly folded,
yet to be unfurled.
Fresh from sleeping,
fresh from dreaming,
come from heaven above,
we to whom you have been given,
bring you all our love.

MERYL DONEY, TWENTIETH CENTURY

THE CHRISTENING

A light in the world

Thank you, Father, that today our baby has been signed with the sign of your cross.

May he/she not be ashamed to confess the faith of Christ crucified and to fight valiantly under his banner against sin, the world and the devil. May he/she continue Christ's faithful soldier and servant to the end of his/her life.

Thank you Father for the candle we received today. May our baby son/daughter shine as a light in the world to your glory.

BASED ON THE BOOK OF COMMON PRAYER

BABY'S DEDICATION

A prayer of dedication

This is ....
We thank God for him/her.
We offer him/her back to God.
We pray for him/her and all his/her family.
We welcome him/her into this family of believers.

Welcome to the family

Father, we thank you that you have given us families. May this child grow up surrounded by our love.

Thank you, too, that we belong to the wider family of your church. May this child grow up among those who love and serve you.

A CONFIRMATION

The Confirmation prayer

Defend, O Lord, this thy child (*or* this thy servant) with thy heavenly grace, that he/she may continue thine for ever; and daily increase in the Holy Spirit, more and more, until he/she come unto thy everlasting kingdom.

FROM THE BOOK OF COMMON PRAYER

The work of faith

May God make you worthy of the life he has called you to live. May he fulfil by his power all your desire for goodness and complete your work of faith. In this way the name of our Lord Jesus will receive glory from you, and you from him, by the grace of our God and of the Lord Jesus Christ.

BASED ON THE SECOND LETTER TO THE THESSALONIANS, CHAPTER 1

A WEDDING

A wedding prayer

Almighty God, our heavenly Father,
who gave marriage to be a source of blessing to mankind,
we thank you for the joys of family life.
May we know your presence and peace in our homes;
fill them with your love,
and use them for your glory;
though Jesus Christ our Lord.

FROM THE ALTERNATIVE SERVICE BOOK

The gift of marriage

Father, we thank you for the gift of marriage, part of your creation for the strength, comfort and joy of man and woman.

Lord Jesus, thank you for your presence at a wedding when you were on earth and for the wine of happiness you provided for everyone there.

Holy Spirit, thank you for your work of peace and harmony in the lives of God's people.

May these two know your love, Father, your grace, Lord Jesus, and your fellowship, Holy Spirit, from this day forward and for evermore.

MARY BATCHELOR, TWENTIETH CENTURY

A FUNERAL

Entrusted to his love

O God, whose beloved Son took children into his arms and blessed them, give us grace to entrust .... to your never-failing care and love, and bring us all to your heavenly kingdom; through Jesus Christ our Lord, who lives and reigns with you and the Holy Spirit, one God, now and for ever.

FROM THE ALTERNATIVE SERVICE BOOK

Death is only an horizon

We give back to you, O God, those whom you gave to us. You did not lose them when you gave them to us and we do not lose them by their return to you.

Your dear Son has taught us that life is eternal and love cannot die, so death is only an horizon and an horizon is only the limit of our sight. Open our eyes to see more clearly and draw us close to you that we may know that we are nearer to our loved ones, who are with you. You have told us that you are preparing a place for us; prepare us also for that happy place, that where you are we may also be always, O dear Lord of life and death.

BASED ON WILLIAM PENN, SEVENTEENTH CENTURY

CHILDREN'S PRAYERS

Jesus our friend

Jesus, friend of little children,
be a friend to me;
take my hand and ever keep me
close to thee.

W.J. MATHAMS, NINETEENTH CENTURY

For the morning

Father, we thank you for the night,
and for the pleasant morning light;
for rest and food and loving care,
and all that makes the day so fair.

Help us to do the things we should,
to be to others kind and good;
in all we do at work or play,
to grow more loving every day.

REBECCA J. WESTON

For creation

All things bright and beautiful,
all creatures great and small,
all things wise and wonderful,
the Lord God made them all.

He gave us eyes to see them,
and lips that we might tell,
how great is God Almighty,
who has made all things well.

CECIL FRANCIS ALEXANDER, NINETEENTH CENTURY

For all creatures

Dear Father, hear and bless
your beasts and singing birds;
and guard with tenderness
small things that have no words.

EDITH RUTTER LEATHAM, TWENTIETH CENTURY

Be near me

Be near me, Lord Jesus, I ask thee to stay
close by me for ever, and love me, I pray.
Bless all the dear children in thy tender care;
and fit us for heaven to live with thee there.

JOHN MCFARLAND

God is strong and wise

God, our loving father, thank you that you never change.
You are as strong and wise and loving as the day you
made the world. Thank you that nothing can ever happen that
will make you alter. You are the one true God and Maker of all.
We worship you in Jesus' name.

ZINNIA BRYAN, TWENTIETH CENTURY

Watch my sleep

Jesus, tender Shepherd, hear me,
bless your little lamb tonight;
through the darkness please be near me,
watch my sleep till morning light.

MARY LUNDIE DUNCAN, NINETEENTH CENTURY

Goodnight

Good night! Good night!
Far flies the light;
but still God's love
shall flame above,
making all bright.
Good night! Good night!

VICTOR HUGO, NINETEENTH CENTURY

Graces

Thank you for the world so sweet,
thank you for the food we eat,
thank you for the birds that sing,
thank you, God, for everything.

EDITH RUTTER LEATHAM, TWENTIETH CENTURY

For what we are about to receive,
may the Lord make us truly grateful.

AUTHOR UNKNOWN

For every cup and plateful,
God make us truly grateful.

AUTHOR UNKNOWN

Come, Lord Jesus, be our guest,
and may our meal by you be blest.

ATTRIBUTED TO MARTIN LUTHER, SIXTEENTH CENTURY

Bless, O Lord, this food to our use and bless us to your
service, and make us ever mindful of the needs of others;
through Jesus Christ our Lord.

AUTHOR UNKNOWN

Bless me, O Lord, and let my food strengthen me to serve thee, for Jesus Christ's sake.

ISAAC WATTS, EIGHTEENTH CENTURY

Praise God, from whom all blessings flow,
praise him, all creatures here below,
praise him above, you heavenly host
praise Father, Son and Holy Ghost.

THOMAS KEN, SEVENTEENTH CENTURY

To God who gives our daily bread
a thankful song we raise,
and pray that he who sends us food
may fill our hearts with praise.

THOMAS TALLIS, SIXTEENTH CENTURY

Be present at our table, Lord,
be here and everywhere adored:
thy creatures bless, and grant that we
may feast in paradise with thee.

JOHN CENNICK, EIGHTEENTH CENTURY

BLESSINGS

Moses' blessing on the children of Israel

The Lord bless thee,
and keep thee:
the Lord make his face shine upon thee,
and be gracious unto thee:
the Lord lift up his countenance upon thee,
and give thee peace.

FROM THE BOOK OF NUMBERS, CHAPTER 6

Paul's blessing on the church at Rome

May the God of hope fill you with all joy and peace as you trust in him, so that you may overflow with hope by the power of the Holy Spirit.

FROM THE LETTER TO THE ROMANS, CHAPTER 15

And for the church at Corinth

May the grace of the Lord Jesus Christ, and the love of God, and the fellowship of the Holy Spirit be with us all, evermore.

BASED ON THE SECOND LETTER TO THE CORINTHIANS, CHAPTER 13

Celtic blessings

May the road rise to meet you.
May the wind be always at your back.
May the sun shine warm upon your face.
May the rains fall softly upon your fields
and, until we meet again,
may God hold you in the hollow of his hand.

Celtic blessing

Deep peace

Peace of the running waves to you,
Deep peace of the flowing air to you,
Deep peace of the quiet earth to you,
Deep peace of the shining stars to you,
Deep peace of the shades of night to you,
Moon and stars always giving light to you,
Deep peace of Christ, the Son of Peace, to you.

Celtic blessing

Bless unto me

Do thou, O God, bless unto me
each thing mine eye doth see;
do thou, O God, bless unto me
each sound that comes to me;
do thou, O God, bless unto me
each savour that I smell;
do thou, O God, bless unto me
each taste in mouth doth dwell;
each sound that goes unto my song,
each ray that guides my way,
each thing that I pursue along,
each lure that tempts to stray,
the zeal that seeks my living soul,
the Three that seek my heart and whole,
the zeal that seeks my living soul,
the Three that seek my heart and whole.

AN EARLY SCOTTISH BLESSING

God give us light

May God give us light to guide us, courage to support us,
and love to unite us, now and evermore.

AUTHOR UNKNOWN

DOXOLOGIES OF
PRAISE TO GOD

Holy, holy, holy, is the Lord God Almighty, who was, who is, and who is to come.

FROM THE BOOK OF REVELATION, CHAPTER 4

Blessing and glory and wisdom
and thanksgiving and honour and power and might
be to our God for ever and ever!

FROM THE BOOK OF REVELATION, CHAPTER 7

Glory be to thee, O Lord,
Glory to thee, O holy One,
Glory to thee, O King!

ST JOHN CHRYSOSTOM, FOURTH CENTURY

O all ye works of the Lord,
bless ye the Lord:
praise him and magnify him for ever.

FROM THE BOOK OF COMMON PRAYER

Creation's praise

May none of God's wonderful works
keep silence, night or morning.
Bright stars, high mountains, the depths of the seas,
sources of rushing rivers:
May all these break into song as we sing
to Father, Son and Holy Spirit.
May all the angels in the heavens reply:
Amen! Amen! Amen!
Power, praise, honour, eternal glory
to God, the only giver of grace.
Amen! Amen! Amen!

A DOXOLOGY FROM EGYPT, THIRD CENTURY

Blessing and honour

Blessing and honour and thanksgiving and praise, more than
we can utter, more than we can conceive, be unto thee,
O holy and glorious Trinity, Father, Son, and Holy Ghost, by
all angels, by all men, and all creatures, for ever and ever.

THOMAS KEN, SEVENTEENTH CENTURY

Praise to the trinity

To God the Father, who first loved us,
and made us accepted in the beloved:
to God the Son, who loved us,
and washed us from our sins in his own blood:
to God the Holy Ghost, who sheds the love of God
abroad in our hearts:
be all love and all glory,
for all time and for eternity.

THOMAS KEN, SEVENTEENTH CENTURY

O being of life

O Being of life!
O Being of peace!
O Being of time,
and time without cease!
O Being, infinite, eternity!
O Being, infinite, eternity!

PRAYER FROM THE ISLAND OF BENBECULA

God

God
within
and without.

God
underground and overground
everywhere and nowhere
always and never
sometimes and all times.

God
inside
and
outside.

God
here
with
us
now.

MARTIN WROE, TWENTIETH CENTURY

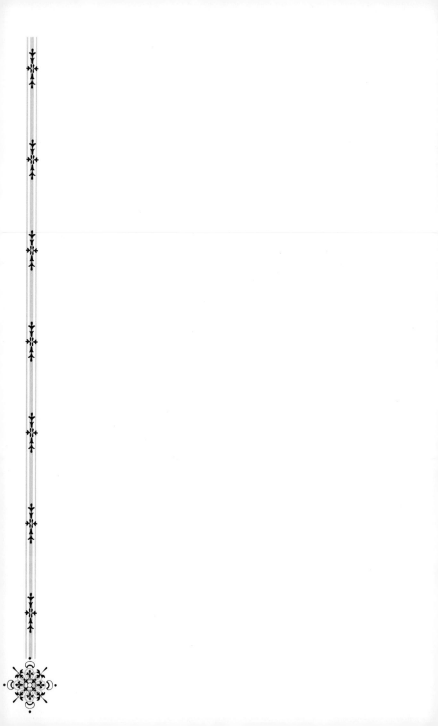

Index of First Lines

Index of Sources

ACKNOWLEDGMENTS

Verse one of 'Jesus, Friend of Little Children' by W.J. Mathams (1853–1931) reprinted by permission of Oxford University Press.

'Father, we thank you for the gift of marriage' by Mary Batchelor. Copyright © Mary Batchelor. Used by permission of William Neill-Hall Ltd.

'God give us rain when we expect sun' from *A Common Prayer* by Michael Leunig. Used with permission of Ivor Cutler.

'God / Underground and overground' by Martin Wroe. Used by permission of Martin Wroe.

'O God, it is so hard for us' by Monica Furlong. Reproduced by permission of the author.

Extract from *My God and King: Prayers of Christian Devotion* by Frank Colquhoun. Copyright © SPCK.

Extracts reproduced from *Justice and Mercy* by Reinhold Niebuhr edited by Ursula M. Niebuhr. Copyright © 1974 Ursula M. Niebuhr. Published by Westminster John Knox Press.

Mrs Edith Rutter Leatham, 'Dear Father, hear and bless' and 'Thank you for the world so sweet', reproduced from *Further Everyday Prayers* by permission of the National Christian Education Council.

'Bless our beautiful land, O Lord' spoken by Archbishop Desmond Tutu at the inauguration of Nelson Mandela as State President of South Africa in Pretoria in 1994.

'Broken Friendships' copyright © Kathy Keay. Reprinted from *Laughter, Silence and Shouting* (HarperCollins) by permission of the estate of Kathy Keay.

'O God of integrity' copyright © Janet Morley and 'Christian Aid Prayer', published by Christian Aid.

Prayers from *The Alternative Service Book 1980* are copyright © The Central Board of Finance of the Church of England and are reproduced by permission.

'The Reconciliation Prayer' copyright © Coventry Cathedral, 1964. Reprinted with permission of Coventry Cathedral.

'I am only a spark' from Mexico in *Prayers for Mission*. Copyright © The United Society for the Propagation of the Gospel.